THE GARDENS AT GIVERNY

MONET'S PASSION

Photographs by Elizabeth Murray ❦ Address Book

Pomegranate

SAN FRANCISCO

Published by Pomegranate Communications, Inc.
Box 6099, Rohnert Park, California 94927

Pomegranate Europe, Ltd.
Fullbridge House, Fullbridge
Maldon, Essex CM9 4LE, England

ISBN 0-7649-0039-0
Catalog No. A872

Elizabeth Murray is the author of *Monet's Passion: Ideas, Inspiration and Insights
from the Painter's Gardens* (Pomegranate Artbooks), and her work is featured in
an annual calendar, *Monet's Passion,* and a book of postcards, *Monet's Gardens at
Giverny,* also published by Pomegranate. She currently resides in northern
California. Murray makes her living as a garden designer, garden writer, and
photographer and travels extensively giving lectures on garden design and
Claude Monet's gardens at Giverny.

Cover photograph:
Apple-blossom-pink geraniums and 'Queen Elizabeth' standard roses in
monochromatic island beds in front of Claude Monet's house

Back cover photograph:
Monet's pink stucco house, accented with green shutters
and a rose-covered trellis

Title page:
Claude Monet in his garden, c. 1923
Photograph courtesy Musée Claude Monet

Designed by Harrah Argentine

Printed in Korea

05 04 03 02 01   10 9 8 7 6 5

THE LEGENDARY FRENCH IMPRESSIONIST CLAUDE MONET believed his gardens to be his artistic masterpiece. He lived in Giverny for the last forty years of his life, and his gardens there became not only the subject of most of his paintings but also his own private "controlled laboratories" where he could experiment with color, texture, light, and shadow.

Garden designer Elizabeth Murray worked as a gardener on the restored Giverny estate for a year and has firsthand knowledge of and thorough insight into Monet's own garden planning, color palette, and seasonal plantings. Her expertise is reflected in this outstanding selection of forty color photographs of the flower and water gardens at Giverny featuring the famous Grand Allée, tulip beds, and waterlily pond with Japanese footbridge.

Elizabeth Murray is the author of *Monet's Passion: Ideas, Inspiration and Insights from the Painter's Gardens* (Pomegranate Artbooks, 1989), and her work is featured in an annual calendar, *Monet's Passion,* also published by Pomegranate. She currently resides in northern California. Murray makes her living as a garden designer, garden writer, and photographer and travels extensively giving lectures on garden design and Claude Monet's gardens at Giverny. ❧

In front of Monet's house at Giverny, red and pink tulips burst
through a sea of vivid blue forget-me-nots. In the foreground, spears
of purple bearded iris, mounds of golden English wallflowers, and a
border of lilac aubrieta provide a regal color combination.

Elegant clusters of delicate pink roses harmonize with the pink
stucco walls of Monet's house; deep red roses and lush green foliage
provide a pleasing counterpoint.

Jewellike pink-and-white waterlilies sparkle on the surface of
the reflecting pond. Monet insisted that the pond be kept clear
as a mirror and that the spreading waterlily pads be trimmed in
circular patterns.

The water garden's glassy surface became a liquid canvas on which Monet manipulated shapes, colors, and textures. Here, floating waterlilies and reflections of trees and foliage, enhanced by the blue of the sky and the white of passing clouds, create a dazzling multidimensional effect.

The thirteen-foot-high arches of the Grand Allée, the main axis of
Monet's Clos Normand flower garden, support a fragrant profusion
of rambling roses. Lacy lilac aubrieta edges the flowerbeds below,
accenting the roses' delicate hue.

Shimmering in the sun, a burst of fiery red blooms floats on a sea of green, mauve, purple, and white.

Deep red Oriental poppies *(Papaver orientale)* with velvety black
centers contrast nicely with soft pink sweet william and snowy white
Shasta daisies along this garden path.

Monet's famed waterlily pond, mirroring the sky and surrounding
foliage, treats the eye to a natural impressionistic masterpiece. In the
background, lavender and white wisteria crown the graceful
Japanese footbridge.

The brilliant red petals and graceful stems and pods of Oriental
poppies add interest to this cluster of lacy lavender blooms.

Monet's pink stucco house is accented with green shutters and a rose-covered trellis that runs the length of the porch. The blue-and-white-curtained French door leads to Monet's kitchen, from which trays of food were often carried to the garden for family picnics.

Clusters of sunny yellow flag iris brighten the edges of Monet's waterlily pond. On the far side of the pond, the large, distinctive leaves of sweet coltsfoot *(Petasites japonicus)* echo the shapes of the floating waterlily pads.

In autumn, trailing orange and gold nasturtiums spill from their beds
and take over the path beneath the Grand Allée while a robust
profusion of blooms bursts from the seven-foot-wide borders.

Hot pink cosmos *(Cosmos bipinnatus)* and white-tipped dahlias seem
to float above an airy, delicate stand of white rose asters.

A delightful jumble of bearded iris in predominantly rosy purple,
lavender blue, and starry white is neatly edged by soft mounds of
lilac aubrieta. Flames of crimson Oriental poppies boldly punctuate
these cool colors.

This garden path treats the eye to a stunning potpourri of vivid
pink and lavender blooms framed by an intricate network of
lacy green foliage.

Monet's water garden tapestry is woven with many textures, shapes, and hues. Here, yellow, white, and acid green tones mingle with the dappled reflections of blue sky glimpsed through a lacy curtain of deep green foliage.

In the misty light of dawn, brilliantly hued flower heads and
swordlike foliage seem to reach out to meet over this garden path.

A drift of showy pink and mauve tulips echoes the hue of Monet's
pink stucco house.

L

Fifi, the calico cat who lives in Monet's garden, pauses beneath a fiery blaze of golden English wallflowers and red-and-white tulips.

L

Sweet rocket *(Hesperis matronalis)* highlights a lovely view of the
waterlily pond.

The brilliant sunlight of a spring morning illuminates Monet's garden
in a blaze of yellow, gold, and acid green hues.

M

A monochromatic island flower bed of soft pink tulips and rose-colored English daisies *(Bellis perennis)* is planted in front of Monet's house, repeating its color scheme of pink and green.

N

This charming and practical rowboat has been used for more
than a century by the many gardeners who have tended the
waterlily pond. Monet himself used the boat for closer study of
his beloved waterlilies.

N

Old-fashioned pink peonies and foxglove mingle harmoniously with
bearded iris in the shade of an apple tree.

O

On the edge of the waterlily pond, lilac puffs of meadow rue
(Thalictrum aquilegifolium) dance with graceful spikes of blue-and-
white lupine above the distinctive heart-shaped leaves of sweet
coltsfoot *(Petasites japonicus)*.

Monet designed the reflective spaces in his pond as carefully as he
did the surrounding foliage and blooms and floating waterlilies. The
reflections became the primary subject of his later paintings.

On the west side of Monet's garden, fiery orange, gold, bronze, and
copper English wallflowers are planted en masse with ruby red
columbine, pink tulips, and cool blue Dutch iris.

P

Fragrant red roses are trained to cascade over umbrella-like structures, adding height and romance to the garden. Underplanted blooms offer a stunning counterpoint in pink and red-violet hues. The snowy white iris's swordlike foliage adds a geometric green accent to the border.

Masses of pink peonies and roses repeat the hues of Monet's stucco
house and fill the air with their heady fragrance.

Morning mist softens the view of Monet's waterlily pond.
The water garden remains as inspiring today as it was for the
great painter himself.

An island of yellow flag iris adds an elegant grace to the
waterlily pond.

S

Below Monet's bedroom window, clusters of fragrant roses tower
over beds of delicate pink geraniums.

A second-story window in Monet's house offers a sweeping vista of the garden in all its springtime splendor. Roses reach out over the arches of the Grand Allée; soon their abundant blooms will fill the air with fragrance.

T

Along the Grand Allée, a bowing sunflower tops a tapestry of purple and rose pink asters interwoven with red cactus dahlias and golden helianthus and accented with the round disks of nasturtium leaves.

Vividly hued peonies and Oriental poppies mingle with pink sweet
william in front of Monet's house. The sweet william gently echoes
the tones of the pink stucco walls.

UV

UV

Above the waterlily pond, a lacy canopy of intermingled white
and lavender wisteria gracefully veils the trellis over the arched
Japanese footbridge.

Purple cranesbill geranium and Siberian iris highlight the edge of the waterlily pond. The round shapes of the waterlily leaves are harmoniously echoed in the leaves of *Petasites japonicus* to the right and in the waterlily pads themselves, stretching back as far as the eye can see.

A profusion of fragrant pink roses stretches over the arches of the Grand Allée, accented by the delicate border of lilac aubrieta at the edge of the gravel path below.

Apple-blossom-pink geraniums and 'Queen Elizabeth' standard roses
are planted in monochromatic island beds in front of Monet's pink
stucco house; nearby beds are planted in red geraniums. Monet's
original color scheme combined pink and red in the same bed,
creating a blend of color similar to that in a pointillist painting.

Viewed through a vibrant stand of blue-violet and pink
Siberian irises, floating waterlily blossoms adorn the surface
of the reflecting pond.